Poetry
by Milagros Rivera

Copyright © 2025 Milagros Rivera
All rights reserved
First Edition

NEWMAN SPRINGS PUBLISHING
320 Broad Street
Red Bank, NJ 07701

First originally published by Newman Springs Publishing 2025

ISBN 978-1-68498-472-5 (Paperback)
ISBN 978-1-68498-473-2 (Digital)

Printed in the United States of America

To herself, her children, and grandchildren,
and great grandchildren

Frustration

April 12, 2017, 12:30 p.m.

How do you deal with your frustration? I would like to talk to someone, but no one is interested in my frustration. So many people say they care, but only when it's convenient for them or when they gain something. I guess nothing is for free but your speech—my actions speak louder than my words, so why is Rodney in so much doubt? What decision do I have to make? Leave that relationship alone. No good is going to come out. No trust. No communication. He can never see the good, only negative. The reactions I have made through my own frustration are with myself, most of all for not saying what I need to say to keep peace where there is none. Fuck it all!

A September Poem

September 6, 2011

What a beautiful month to celebrate,
to acknowledge the number ninth month of
the year. Late summer, the beginning of
fall to get ready for winter.

September is blessed with victory, grace,
mercy; the colors of September then end
to a new beginning, to embrace, to
cherish, to slave, to value, to hold,
and to never let go. To be in
September is to reinvent self to
follow through to October, to fold and
never fold. To share and give and
receive. To be kind and gentle, to nurture
with the month of September to have for
eternity. In every year, we celebrate
September, this month of growth.

Good, Orderly Direction

January 1, 2005, 3:00 p.m.

Thank you, God, for choosing me to be
part of the good, orderly direction.
You have shown me how through
your people of God. Thank you for allowing
me to tap in the good fight. You have
been fighting since God creation.
Thank you for forgiving me and
allowing me to forgive myself and others.
Thank you for allowing me to be
me. Through all your blessing, I am
able to identify me, my own personality,
my own way of coping and going through life.
Being blessed is a gift God allows.
Everyone I see and hear is beyond me.
God's gifts blessed me to use my
gifts to share and care no matter what.
To love as God does is a gift.
He has allowed me to see the difference.

Thought for Today

February 22, 2014, 3:30 p.m.

Ask for what you need, not want.
Embrace someone, encourage them.
Empower someone today
with nations, not words
inspire someone to accept their
talents, big or small.

Embrace

Let your love, trust, grace, mercy
embrace others to change the
hate. To love, to understand,
rather than be understood.

Thought for Today

Ask for what you need not want.
Embrace someone encourage them.
Empower someone today.
With actions not words
Inspire someone to accepts their
Talents big or small.

                Embrace

Let your love, trust, grace, mercy
Embrace others to change the
hate. To love to understand
Rather than be understood.

                                  Milagros Rivera

Dreams
Inspiration
Discover
of
Oneself

September 6, 2017, 1:00 a.m.

To excavate, to dig deep
down within. To hear the
echoes of your past. "Do you hide?"
No, you face the past, present, future
with enthusiasm, happiness,
joyfulness, willingness to change what
you can.

Poem Your Celebration

May 5, 2018, 6:05 p.m.

How do you express your celebration?
I express my celebration by showing my
son happiness, truth, being open-minded
willingness, honesty, freedom.
You are my celebration. I am your
celebration. I express my celebration
with bubbles and balloons.

The Colors of a Rainbow, a Pathway through My Life

March 19, 2019, 5:00 a.m.

The colors of a rainbow, how beautiful.
There is red for my blood; brown is for
the color of my skin. Purple is my willingness
to keep moving forward, no matter what!
Blue is my beautiful sky; white is my
heaven. Black is my dark side; gray is
my shadow. Pink is my open-mindness.
Turquoise is my honesty. Burgundy is my
faith; yellow is my courage. The pathways
through my life is so colorful, like
a rainbow in the sky.

Happy, Joyous, and Free

June 8, 2019, 3:00 a.m.

(Mine and yours) Happy, joyous, and free
to express me, to celebrate me, to
dedicate, to motivate oneself to change,
to embrace it! To grow with it, your
mind, body, and soul. Spirit to be 100 percent
with yourself. Imagination to create, to
learn. Your talent, your creativity to share
is as a gift from God. Instilled in me
to be happy, joyous, and free.
Still happy, joyous, and free—
my motto, no matter what.
Life comes with a lot of
surprises. I am grateful
for the people God put in
my life's path to teach me
honor, value, moral character,
passion, compassion. To give
is to receive; to do another
as you would treat yourself.
My words and my action
tells me who I am. I don't
have to lower my standard
or belittle myself so you
can feel good. I have been
around so much sorrow. Some
times my heart breaks when
I can't help. But first I

have to help myself. I give
hope where there's none.
I feel other people's pain.

Today

Today the sky is clear; the
clouds are floating so smooth
with rhythm, colors of all
kinds of (suit). Today is a great day.
I woke up to have another
day. God has blessed me.
To honor is to love; to trust is
to hope and is to have faith. With grace,
mercy, and forgiveness. all God's gifts
he has instilled in me and you. Today,
tap into yourself 100 percent complete, whole.
To be bold is to hold the
foundation my God has given me to
create and continue to change
as life goes on. Today, today
is a blessed day. Give thanks and
praise, sing songs of joy!

A Thought for Today

September 8, 2019, 3:00 pm

My thought for today:
Ask for what you need,
not what you want.

Embrace someone; encourage them.

Empower someone today with
actions, not words.

Inspire someone to accept
their creativity and their talents.

Be happy, joyous, free
to express love.

Celebration

May 22, 2018, 3:35 a.m.

Let's talk about celebration.
What does it mean to you?
To me, it stands or means
favor, passion, compassion.
To respect, to honor, to be
a majestic being of this universe.
To be alive is to be aware.
To be aware takes time
and patience and discipline for one
to become aware of all things,
people, places, situations,
crises. Chase positive or negative.
But when you allow yourself
to be aware, no one can take
it from you. Your awareness
is a celebration of being
mindful to self and others.
To give yourself a celebration of
actions is to celebrate oneself.

A Love Letter to My Children and Grandchildren

April 1, 2019, 1:00 p.m.

The years are flying by,
"my rainbows."

You all are.
Even one of you is a star in your
own right. I love you all.

And
wish I could hold you tight forever.
But it doesn't work that way.

Please remember me when I am
very old, especially if I don't
remember you.

Think of all the times we played
and laughed under skies of blue.
Try to erase all the arguments
and problems we may have had
through the years.
Concentrate on the laughter and not
the tears. Stay strong and trust in
God to help you find your way, and
remember I love you forever and a day!

To Inspire

March 20, 2015, 3:00 a.m.

To inspire oneself to soar,
No matter what, give me
a chance to live, discover,
to love, to trust, to understand
with honor, integrity, respect
for oneself to be able to

learn how to be reasonable for
one self; you cannot truly give
yourself to them with coming 100 percent
to offer is to

An Expression of Love: How Do You Express Your Love?

September 1, 2005
3/14/__, 12:03 a.m.

I express my love with faith, trust, hope willingness, forgiveness, understanding, communication, compassion. My expression of love—you can touch it, feel it, see it, hear it, smell it, taste it.

My expression of love is sharing it with all special people
God has put on this earth for me.

To have compassion, an expression of love, is surprising, without favor for your heart, mind, body, and soul.

To have expression of love is talented with color so wonderful—you sing and praise the Lord, for him all things are possible.

An expression of love is you and me. God the universe.

Love is an expression of joy, happiness, and freedom.

Determination

February 8, 2020, 3:08 p.m.

A poem of determination
What does it mean?
What does it do?
Determination is
all about action.
Plan goals being
materialized in front
of oneself to endure.
Satisfy contentment
to be stable in oneself.

Poem of Celebration

April 30, 2011, 12:01

Let's talk about celebration.
What does celebration mean to you?
To me, it stands for favor, passion, compassion.
To respect, to honor, to be majestic with
the universe. To be alive is to be aware.
To be aware takes time and patience and discipline
for one to become aware of all things, people
places, situations, crises, chaos positive
or negative. But when you have awareness, no
one can take it from you. Your awareness is a
celebration of being mindful to self and others.
To share your celebration of actions to
celebrate oneself.

Without Hate, There Is No Love

October 15, 2019, 10:28 p.m.

Without Truth there are no Lies
Without Struggle there is no Prosperity
Without Hatred there is no Love
Without Compassion there is no Indifference
Without Despair there is no Hope
Without Hate there is no Love
Without Chaos there is no Order
Without Forgiveness there is no Mercilessness
Without Ignorance there is no Understanding
Without Sadness there is no Happiness
Without Frowns there are no Smiles
Without Hate there is no Love
Without Neglect there is no Nurture
Without Peace there is no War
Without Fear there is no Confidence
Without Hate there is no Love

Love or Betrayal

January 30, 2020, 4:30 p.m.

What is love? Kindness,
consideration, forgiveness,
trust, understanding, hope,
faith, charity, honesty, willingness,
open-mindedness, support, love, loyalty,
caring, comfort, no stress.
To accept a person with their good, bad,
ugly, and indifference, acceptance.
What is betrayal?
Distrust, insecurity, lies,
dishonesty, close-mindedness, control,
playing games with a person's
mind and emotions, belittling,
putting down, discomfort, stress,
physical abuse, verbal abuse, emotional abuse,
spiritual abuse.

    When a person has
    to lose themselves to
love another is not love,
that's betrayal. Love is the
antidote to resolve any situations,
crises, to find a solution
or resolution to repair what

ever is going on in their life. To heal
the wounds of a hurtful, abusive,
childhood, chaotic and dysfunctional, is
the saddest thing I had to accept.
That's what it was like. It's sad
when you don't have memories
with siblings or mother or father.

A Poem for All My People in Heaven that God Has Given Them Life and Death

August 10, 2019

To all my familia who have
passed away to a different
existence in the spirit world,
thank you for being in my
life, giving me a familia
to love, to dislike, to
love from a distance, to have, to hold,
to cherish, to play with, to dance with,
to eat with, to cook with, to color with
to dance with, to argue with,
to trust with, to hope with,
to have for a lifetime then
and know to grow.

A Poem for a Lost Soul

January 29, 2021, 2:30 a.m.

Can you guess what happens to
a lost soul? They wander around,
looking for something but never
finding anything. They just
keep wandering and nowhere
to so nowhere to come. It
is a sad thing to see even when
you have experienced somehow loss.
But they're phases, not making
decisions. To me, you don't
have a life, you're not living,
exploring, discovering, having
a journey that's never-ending
In the beginning or end.
To be lost is lonely, sad, angry
miserable, mean, selfish, too much (ego).

Happy Mother's Day to Me!

May 9, 2021, 2:00 p.m.

I love you, Milagros Rivera.
I love the friend in me.
Thank you, God, for taking
away confusion and feeling
lost, no direction. Thank you
for granting me with independence,
with love, caring, coping skills.
God has given to me.
Thank you, God, for allowing me
to love me 100 percent. Allow me to
allow my God to touch me with
all his goodness and kindness.
God is great; thank you for another
day for breathing life unto me,
for allowing me to give a message
of hope, joy, freedom.

God, help me to continue to do
your will. Thank you, God, for
allowing me to look and see, feel, touch
reality, to live like it is your last.
God, thank you for loving me.

A Poem of Personal Responsibility

November 29, 2020, 1:00 p.m.

To have PR, personal responsibility,
is the most amazing, wonderful,
joyous honor. To have PR is
to grow with your age.
It still takes a lot of
praying for willingness to do
the right thing and following them from beginning to end.
Today it gives me responsibility for
me. I am responsible for me.
It takes a lot of healing,
changing discipline, and good order
and direction to get it, but
when you feel great, to be
responsible for yourself is a
gift only God could have
instilled in us, so we
have good orderly direction.
    God.
We all need it. I know I am
still under construction with my
God, grateful for the work. He
has taught me to give me more
than I can give to others but learn how
to say no. It's powerful. Because people or
family, who ever know you, cannot and will not play with.

Poem of Revenge

August 31, 2016, 4:00 a.m.

What is "revenge" to you? (Ask yourself.)
To me, it is doing harm to another
person that has hurt you, intentional or
not. Preme__ why would someone
want to hurt another? What
is the purpose? To think and act out
is horrible for the person doing
the act, and the person who hurt you is
selfish, evil, mean, sad, sorrowful, miserable.
To get (even) wrong! Revenge is not
powerful until you use this energy to
hurt another.

The Gift of Life

January 1, 2021

The gift of life. To
me is to explore, discover,
rediscover oneself, the
whole person from head
to toe, to know self,
to be able to be in my
own skin, to love and nurture
me. To care for me. To
have my own mind to make choices.
Be responsible. For me, learning
personal responsibility is the
key to being happy, joyous, and
free.

My Little Red Pen

September 26, 2019, 7:00 p.m.

How much my little red pen teaches
me to express my inner
thoughts to share wisdom,
experience my strength, my courage,
my hope. For all to share
with universe, to be as one
with the Almighty, to have
blind faith, to believe, to
achieve God's purpose for
your life to be in tune,
in touch. Connected
is so awesome to
learn and to express it.

A Valentine Poem

February 15, 2020, 10:07 p.m.

Today is a heartful
Day to share, care, and bare
it all with that special someone
in your life, to have the victory
of love, to endure, to embrace,
to secure, to hold, to forgive,
to have compassion for the one you
love, to take care of the needs
of mental, emotional, spiritual, physical.
Not the wants—to want that
delicious heart of chocolate filled,
water, caramel taste, to Kama Sutra
all over each other to massage
every part of oneself, to hold,
to cuddle, to fall in love all over again,
to enter Cupid's arrow,

to let that special part, to
feel pleasure, to smell each
other's scent, to turn on the
fore of passion, to make
a memory that will last forever.
So, when that special person is not
there to make that memory
and to remember how good
it feels, smells, and tastes,
close your eyes and remember
your Valentine, the heartbeat
of love, laughter, and life of
eternity.

A Poem of the Month of January

March 28, 2020, 8:07 p.m.

January is the beginning of a
new year. It is the first month of
the year. It represents winter
of the four seasons we have. January
is for pure innocent of God's
gifts to us which he has instilled
in us since birth, the people
born on this month. January
represents the birthstone garnet.
It is a gemstone of January. January 1 to 19
represents the Capricorn, January 20 to
Jan 31 is Aquarius, the sign for
this beginning month. Most energetic and
hardworking people, the Aquarius
is sure to always achieve the
goals. January represents
the snow that falls in the
winter month.

A Poem for the Month of February

February is the second month
of the year. It represents trust and
understanding, God's gifts instilled
in no sense birth. The birthstone
is amethyst. February 1–19 is Aquarius;
February 20–29 is Pisces. The flower is
violet. Aquarius are assertive, original,
humanitarian, independent, easygoing.
Pisces people have a deep sense of
kindness and compassion, highly tuned
in to everything. They have an easygoing,
likable manner, positive people,
sociable, tuned in to other's feelings
in purification. The month of
February is about action, doing,
getting things prepared for the
month of March, which is next
on the calendar.

A Poem for the Month of March

March is the third month of
the calendar. This month is
for forgiveness and gentleness.
This month represents the
birthstone aquamarine. It is
a rich color and a symbol of youth,
health, and hope. From March 1 to 20,
your sign is Pisces. From 21 of March
to 30, you are Aries. Pieces people
born in March are generous, amiable,
positive, natural people. They have
a deep sense; they are generous and
__ and optimistic, ambitious, and
determined. All gifts from God are
instilled at birth. Aries are
passionate, motivated, confident leaders,
cheerful builders.

The Month of April

April is the fourth month on the calendar
that represents spring, flowers
and trees coming back to life.
This month represents birth,
new hope, faith, mercy. Born on
April 1 to 19, you are Aries; from April 20 to
30, you are Taurus. An Aries is
cheerful, passionate, uncomplicated,
confident, motivated leader. The flower
is daisy, symbol of love, truth. Taurus people
are practical, stoic, materialistic,
stubborn. They have beauty, artistry,
hedonism, love of luxury
and comfort. April is the month of
ongoing growth for people born on
this month to be __ with
God's gifts instilled at birth.
The birthstone is diamonds.

The Month of May

May is the fifth calendar month of the year; flower for May is lily of valley. May 1–20, you are Taurus; you are Gemini if you were born 21–31 of May. A Taurus is ruled by the planet Venus. They are are an Earth's, so determined, ambitious, practical. May represents the bloom of a new growth to earth; it also represents forgiveness, grace, honor, truth. Gemini are adaptable, outgoing, intelligent, indecisive, impulsive, unreable, and nosy. The month of May is the beginning of spring, the second season of the year. The birthstone is emerald.

The Month of June

This is the sixth month of
the calendar. The flower for
this month is rose; it represents
happiness, love, abundance.
People born June 1 to 20 are Gemini,
social, talkative, outgoing.
June 21 to 30, you are a Cancer,
highly intuitive, sensitive,
highly in tune with people,
energetic, extremely self-protective.
The month of June is the
month of happiness. Love
and abundance in all areas
of one life to give back to
receive the gifts God instilled
in the people. Those born in June are
blessed in goodness and are
goddesses of marriage.

The Month of July

The seventh month of the
calendar year. The flower is
larkspur. It represents wisdom.
The month of July also represents
knowledge, discernment, beauty.
The birthstone is ruby.
No-bitchy passion and value. If
you're born in July 1–22, you
are Cancer, highly intuitive,
self-protective. They have the ability
to pick up energies in a room.
They have psychic abilities.
July represents honor, nobility.
The Leo sign represents
warm, dynamic, charismatic, strong
brave, dominant, ready, passionate people.
They delight in opportunity.

The Month of August

The eighth month, the beginning
of summer, the third season in
our world. The people born in
August 1–22 are Leo—
enthusiastic, generous, confident
arrogant. They care too much of
what others think of them. The flows
is gladious and poppy. The August
months also represent understanding,
forgiveness, hope. If you born on
August 22–31, you are Virgo,
hardworking, critical thinkers.
They are patient, faithful;
they are responsible, sweet. They
remember everything. The month
of August also represents
God's gifts of honor, courage,
hope, trust, confidence.

The Month of September

September is the ninth month of
The calendar year. The flower is
aster and morning glory, a symbol
of all-powerful love, affection, and
wisdom. The beginning of autumn
season, it represents
refocus, valor, faith. September 12–3,
you are Virgo, September 24–31, Libra.
Virgo are hardworking, patient;
they remember everything. They are
amazing artists, faithful, responsible.
If you are Libra, cool, calculating,
cerebral, charming, swift, humorous,
good company, balanced, clever.
The month of September also
represents hope, love, balance,
greatness, courage that God
has instilled since birth.
Birthstone is sapphire.

The Month of October

October is the tenth month on
the calendar. The flower is
opal element. Our symbol
is scales. The month of October
represents the last season of the month
of fall, where the trees change color
to let you know they are about change.
If you were born October 1–22, you
are Libra. People are passionate,
brave, diplomatic, social, chase
justice, indecisive, self-pity,
cruel, grief, jealous. October 23–31, you are a Scorpio.
Success-driven, they are resilient, incredible people,
fire sign, passionate for power, emotional,
extremely clairvoyant, and
intuitive. They have willpower and determination.

The Month of November

The month of November
is the eleventh month in the year.
To celebrate November is
to smile, to laugh, to
be in autumn waiting for
winter to come upon the
Earth. See the trees
change colors, bright red, orange,
brown. To see November
is to be aware and alive,
to feel the breeze. God
has granted you to hold and
embrace all beautiful they of
November.

My Thought for This Day

November 23, 2020, 4:03 p.m.

Thank you, God, for
allowing me to heal the past
wounds that used to keep me
stuck down, sad, angry, bitter, hateful.
Thank you, God, for sending me your
people to teach me your will, and
one day, our wills will be together as
one, as you intended for me, your
wonderful daughter, Milagros Castillo, a.k.a. Milagros Rivera.

My Thought for This Day

September 25, 2019, 10:30 p.m.

Thank God for allowing me
To keep growing in my mind,
body, soul, and spirit. There are
so many areas still under construction
that God will allow me to tap in
and explore, discover, and rediscover.

My Thought for the Day

October 1, 2011, 6:30 p.m.

Thank you, God, for your
direction and guidance. I am
learning to appreciate all things on
earth you have created for your people
and everything you are teaching me,
to shine and care for others and give.
God's love is unconditional, forever,
pure 100 percent genuine. Thank you,
God, for loving me and choosing
me to continue your good.
I am grateful I am still
under your construction, Lord.
I will sing and praise you
All the days of my life.
I will continue to tap
to your precious gifts of life
to live, learn, laugh, love.
All your gifts are given
To us at birth.

My Thought for Today

January 19, 2021, 9:00 p.m.

Be grateful for this
day God has allowed
us to have, have old, to cherish.

Poem of the Harvest Moon on Halloween Eve

October 30, 2020, 9:21 p.m.

As I rode down the
street, I spotted the
beautiful moon that God
has offered me. His beautiful
picture of sky clouds is gone.
Clear sky and giant harvest moon
are looking at you as you
glance at the beautiful image.
God has offered you this
day to __ life
Thanksgiving light.

A Birthday Poem for My Hero Affinity

September 6, 2020

She was born September 13, 2019. She will be one year old. For the first eight months of her life, she had been hospitalized. She has had to battle many things, and she has overcome them through the grace of God. She is my hero, Affinity Joanna. I am honored to be her great-great auntie. She is so beautiful. She is blessed. I am proud I have an opportunity to be in her life. I love her so much. Happy first birthday, my hero, and many more to come.

Poem Affinity

God's grace is with her. She is so awesome; I am happy to participate in her life. I was blessed with my hero on September 13, 2019. She was born to the world so she can shine bright as a star. Her yellow skin is like the sunshine. Her brown eyes are so big and beautiful. I see great things for the present and future. I have been blessed to be by her side. Even when I am not there,

we have a beautiful connection.
My hero will soar like the
birds in the sky. She will roar
like the lioness and queen she is.
I am so honored to be her
tia. Affinity Joanne, such a
beautiful name. She looks like
her mother, Carmen, and her grandma
Joann. She is so special in
all areas of her life. We will
continue to love her, nurture her,
care for her, protect her. Love you, my
hero.
    Love you,
        Nana-tia
            Milly.

www.ingramcontent.com/pod-product-compliance
Lightning Source LLC
Chambersburg PA
CBHW031658040426
42453CB00006B/340